AND SO I DID

Marjorie Lamson

ATHENA PRESS
LONDON

AND SO I DID
Copyright © Marjorie Lamson 2004

All Rights Reserved

No part of this book may be reproduced in any form
by photocopying or by any electronic or mechanical means,
including information storage or retrieval systems,
without permission in writing from both the copyright
owner and the publisher of this book.

ISBN 1 84401 209 3

First Published 2004 by
ATHENA PRESS
Queen's House, 2 Holly Road
Twickenham TW1 4EG

Printed for Athena Press

AND SO I DID

Dedicated to my children, Howard and Mary

Prologue

'You're off on one of your foreign trips tomorrow,' our friends said, 'so we'd better leave you to get packed. Where are you going to this time, by the way?'

'We're going to a place called Damme in Germany.'

'Why do you always seem to choose places we've never heard of?'

'We didn't choose it this time, my cousin John and his wife Mary Ann, who live in America, are flying over to join us. Mary Ann's father's family came from Damme and she wants to look for family connections. They invited us to join them because they've never been to Germany, but we know it well. When they have finished their researching in Damme we plan to go on a round tour.'

'We didn't know you had American connections.'

'I was born in America, but that's a long story. One day I shall write it down.'

And so I did…

My mother was English. She married an American serviceman who had been serving in Europe during the First World War. When he returned to the United States she went with him and they started to raise a family. Their first-born was my elder sister, Kathleen, and I followed. I was born on 31st October – Halloween – in Boston, Massachusetts. My mother, claiming homesickness, decided to take a 'holiday' in England, taking her two children with her. She was already pregnant when she left America, and my younger sister, Patricia, was born in England.

Although my mother's trip to England was supposed to be only temporary she never returned to the United States, despite appeals from my father and his family. Instead she remarried and I acquired a stepfather. At the age of three I had surgery on my neck at the Great Ormond Street Hospital for Sick Children, where my maternal grandmother worked as a doctor's assistant. To recuperate after the operation I was sent to stay with my grandmother for a few weeks. I had a very happy time there but had to return to my mother.

I decided that I preferred life with my grandmother. I was most unhappy at my mother's house and one day left home, taking my younger sister with me. Our ages were four and three years. We were found wandering in Chelsea by a policeman and were returned to our mother's home, whereupon I refused to eat until I got my wish to live with my grandmother. I stayed with her until I married.

The years passed and the Second World War started. I joined the London Auxiliary Ambulance Service and went through the war years in London. I met Bill and we were married. After our first child, Howard, was born, I decided that I would make a real effort to trace my father's family and, if possible, my father himself.

I would have been about one year old when I left America, too young to have recorded any clear memories. Nevertheless, for as long as I can remember, I had felt a strong affinity with my father, and as I grew up I became determined to locate and, if possible, meet him. I wonder if this could have been an example of the phenomenon now recognised and known as bonding, which had occurred in the first few months of my life.

The following is an account of the adventures which led to the discovery, one by one, of a whole host of relatives but which, unfortunately, failed in the ultimate objective, which was to meet with my father. With virtually no clues to go on, I thought, Where shall I start? No good going to the Public Records Office in London; there would be nothing there. I would have to contact sources in the United States. After consideration I concluded that if my father were still alive, he would be paying taxes.

My first line of enquiry, therefore, would be to the US Treasury Department. I asked if they could supply a list of people named Lamson (family name) in the New England and Midwest areas. I also wrote to the Vehicle Licensing Department, mailed the letters and awaited results. In the meantime I wrote to the Boston Family Society. At last the wheels had been set in motion.

Weeks passed and no acknowledgements came. Then, one morning an envelope with the US Treasury logo landed on the doormat. My heart leapt in anticipation of what it might contain. With trembling fingers and a small frisson of excitement, I opened the envelope to be confronted by a short note of acknowledgement and a list of some twenty-five names of Lamsons. Eagerly, I scanned down to see if a

Clarence Everett (my father's first names) was included. The name was not there – but wait, there was one that attracted my attention, namely Everett C. Lamson. Surely, I thought, that would be an interesting lead to follow.

A letter was duly sent to Everett C. Lamson. I sat back once again to await results. The reply, when it came, was interesting, and held out a ray of hope for further developments in that he had exhausted all possible leads for me and seemed very keen to help me further in my quest. Going on the information that I had given him, he found that it tallied with a book he had on the Lamson family. What luck! Things were really moving.

In the interim I had received communications from other sources, but nothing concrete, so I decided to concentrate on the contacts mentioned in Everett C. Lamson's letter. After further correspondence he sent me a condensed family tree, which did include my father's name and that of his brothers, one older and one younger, and one sister. Records of the family line beyond that were not included in that volume of the family tree. The condensed family tree did include, however, the names of my paternal grandparents, which confirmed that I had found the right line, all descendants of William Lamson of Ipswich, Mass.

According to further information from Everett C. Lamson, William left England with two brothers in 1634 for America, so we were descendants from the same line. The brothers came from a small village called Ridgewell in Essex. A collateral branch later became the Earls of Durham. That information is contained in a book by the sculptress, Malvina Hoffman, whose mother was a Lamson.

But wait! I am jumping ahead. I had written to the film company, Metro-Goldwyn-Mayer, as, according to my mother, my father had been a cameraman with them before eventually setting up a small film company with a colleague named Lester White. It is not known if the company flourished. Not surprisingly, after all the years, my quest along this route came to a dead end.

Later, I was informed by the US Treasury Department that, whereas there was no record of a Clarence Everett Lamson in the 1960 tax returns, they did have a listing for a Guy Lamson and a Helen Lamson of Avon Lake, Ohio. That was good news, as my mother had mentioned that my father had an elder brother named Guy. Another piece of the jigsaw was in place: very exciting! I intended to write to Guy, but before I could do so I received a letter from Everett C. Lamson informing me that, as a result of further investigations, he had found my father's address. So the final piece of the jigsaw seemed to be in place and all that remained for me to do was to write to that address. I promptly did this and eagerly awaited the outcome, blissfully unaware of the hornet's nest I was about to uncover. Oh dear!

The next letter I received was not from my father, as I had hoped, but from one Louise Henderson who, it transpired, was my father's youngest sister. She had just had a visit from a very distressed Georgia, my father's second wife. Georgia was in absolute ignorance of her husband's previous marriage and the fact that he had children from that marriage. Georgia and Louise were great friends as well as being sisters-in-law, but in view of the devastating news, Georgia dashed to Louise to hear more of the deception and to question why she had not been informed before. Needless to say, it was a most unhappy situation and I was really sorry that I had inadvertently been the bearer of the news. Not knowing that my father had remarried I was so eager to find my roots that all other considerations and possible complications never entered my head.

So what to do? I decided to write to Louise in the hope that she would understand. She replied to my letter and apprised me of other brothers and sisters of Clarence and Guy. Guy was the eldest brother, Louise the youngest sister. In between were twins, Marion and Mildred. Doris, the eldest sister, Marjorie and Elizabeth were the female children. The males were Kenneth, Clarence, Gerald and Guy. One son died in early childhood. Louise also informed me that I had a half-sister, Dorothy, daughter of Georgia. I had 'inherited' a rather large family!

Apparently the whole family had been sworn to secrecy about my father's first marriage, which was, I think, rather unfair to Georgia. It was not surprising that she was absolutely devastated by the news coming to her by way of my letter. I did hope that one day I could meet Georgia and make amends.

My next thought was to plan a visit to the USA to meet my relatives, perhaps learn more about them and possibly actually meet my father. As a prelude to my intended visit my husband, Bill, who, like me, had lost touch with his family, was quite willing to help me in my quest. Although he had no great desire to find his own relatives he was sympathetic to my wishes and genuinely interested in the outcome of my research.

Bill had arranged to make a business trip to Rochester, New York State, in the autumn of 1961, and would have a few days to spare before returning home. He agreed to telephone Everett C. Lamson from Rochester and arrange, if possible, a visit to the Lamsons at their home in Chelsea, Vermont. From now on I shall refer to E. C. Lamson as 'Bud'.

I had written to Bud telling him that my husband would be visiting the United States and would get in touch. Bill accordingly called the Lamson's number in Vermont and the conversation went something like this:

Bud: 'Hello, Bud Lamson speaking.'

Bill: 'This is Bill Ball, Marjorie's husband. I'm in

Rochester, New York, on business and have a few days to spare before returning to England. I wondered if it would be convenient to visit you in Chelsea.'

Bud: 'We would be delighted to see you. Our business is such that, if I know ahead, I can take off as much time as is necessary to meet with you. We look forward to seeing you.'

Bill arranged the date and time of his arrival in Chelsea and said goodbye. He duly arrived at the Lamsons' house and was greeted by Bud and his wife, Karleen. Bill says that they were a little cautious at first but quickly seemed to accept that he was the genuine article. He was then entertained, as he says, 'most royally'. After a convivial evening enjoying a superb meal and a not very moderate consumption of Manhattans and Southern Comfort, he retired to bed in a very euphoric frame of mind, thinking that the Lamsons were delightful people and most hospitable – an impression that has stayed with him to this day. No sooner had he dozed off, or so it seemed, he was woken by a vigorous licking from the family pet, a huge German shepherd dog, so obviously it was time to remove himself from the bed. After a splendid and typically American breakfast consisting of crisp bacon, smoked sausages, pancakes and maple syrup, not entirely suitable after the previous night's indulgencies but thoroughly enjoyed nevertheless, he was taken to see an historic locomotive called 'Rock of Ages' in a local granite quarry. Bud was accompanied by his two sons, Jimmy and Karl. They had brought with them a selection of handguns and rifles and the four of them spent the rest of the morning shooting at targets.

After a delightful two days in Vermont it was time for Bill to return home to England. On arrival, he recounted to me the hospitality and genuine warmth shown to him by the Vermont branch of the Lamson family. He brought back with him an invitation to visit again, this time with me, which we hoped to do in the not too distant future. The not too distant future arrived earlier than expected. It brought not our visit to the US but a request from Bud and Karleen for Karl, their youngest son, to spend a few weeks in England as our guest. We were delighted to agree and quite touched by their faith in us to look after Karl so far from home. Howard, our son, and Karl were about the same age, and Mary, our daughter, some four years younger, so it was a good opportunity for the younger generation to get to know each other.

We met Karl at Heathrow Airport. One of his first remarks was on the number of 'WAY OUT' signs he saw. The standard wording in America is 'EXIT'. He was quite amused because 'way out' was a term much in fashion in the US at that time meaning that something was out of the ordinary or odd. Karl noticed quite a lot of differences in the meaning of words while he was with us and said he might compile a little dictionary when he got back to the States. I don't know if he ever did.

That little incident broke the ice and Karl settled down with us very well. Howard showed him around and they took a trip to Scotland together. Bill, who had spent a lot of time in Germany on business, thought it would be rather nice to take Karl to see some of the favourite haunts there including medieval towns like Rothenburg ob der Tauber and Dinkelsbuhl, which were flourishing long before the United States came into existence.

Bill was quite prepared to take Karl to visit Berlin but the latter declined because he had promised his parents not to go behind the 'Iron Curtain'. America was, at that time, very sensitive about anything to do with communism, and Karl's parents would not have been happy at the thought of him travelling through the 'red' territory of East Germany. Instead of visiting Berlin they went on to Austria. In Innsbruck they took a cable car ride up the mountain that overlooks the city from the north. There they met a very pleasant and friendly young French Canadian couple who were touring with a rented Volkswagen and were going on to drive into Northern Italy. They invited Bill and Karl to join them. The four of them drove through the famous Brenner Pass to Vipiteno, the first town in Italy after the border. This pleased Karl very much, as it added another country to his collection of those visited during his European tour.

On the return of Bill and Karl from Europe, we took Karl to various places of interest including Stonehenge, the Tower of London and Stratford-on-Avon. To anyone coming from a country whose recorded history starts in the seventeenth century, the age of these places must be mind-boggling. Karl was prompted to ask, 'Is all England old?' In the Tower of London he noticed a plaque on the wall of a tower with the date nine hundred and something. He thought that the one before the nine had been missed out and took some convincing that the building of the Tower really had begun in the first millennium.

Another place where I took Karl was the then famous roof garden of Derry and Toms, the department store in Kensington, where we had tea in the open air. He was rather concerned that birds flew onto the tea table. Americans were very hygiene conscious at that time and, I think, to a varying extent still are. Karl was very interested in his visits to various museums, particularly the Museum of London which traces the history and development of the capital from prehistoric times to the present day.

After Karl's visit I began to give serious thought to making plans for my first visit to the land of my birth and, possibly, a reunion with my father; but, alas, that meeting was never to take place: so near and yet so far.

A letter from Louise informed me of the death of my father from a massive heart attack. I did ponder the thought that maybe I had indirectly precipitated the attack. This troubled me greatly. I am sure he could not have expected his past to catch up with him after all those years.

I continued to correspond with Louise, who became a lynchpin in my contacts with the family, and I eventually decided to make a visit the following year. The planned visit was to be quite comprehensive in that I had a lot of ground to cover, with relatives in the New England area and the Midwest. But first, Bill and I flew to Boston in the spring of 1969. Karleen Lamson, who drove us to the Lamson's new house in South Barre, Vermont, met us at the airport. From Boston's Logan Airport we drove through Massachusetts and New Hampshire to Vermont, the scenery becoming more and more magnificent as we approached our final destination. I clearly remember stopping off for refreshments at a particularly glorious beauty spot, named Quechee Gorge, just over the border from New Hampshire. It was April and a lot of snow was still lying in Vermont. I could have done with the overcoat that was languishing at home in its plastic cover, having been cleaned for the trip but forgotten in the excitement of preparing for the forthcoming adventure. (I thought of it as we were about to board the plane. I was travelling in a suit, but of course, no turning back – so I had to grin and bear it!)

When we arrived at Bud and Karleen's house, we were welcomed by Bud and their two German shepherd dogs. Bud said that he had been looking forward keenly to meeting his cousin. The dogs decided that we were quite harmless and posed no threat to their territory and we became firm friends. I made a remark that the New England architecture put me in mind of *Peyton Place*, a book and television series that were popular in England at that time. This remark was met rather coldly by Karleen. She probably thought I associated the dubious morals of the book's characters with those of the upstanding inhabitants of South

Barre. She went to great pains to assure me that there was no similarity. The small towns and villages with their white painted clapboard houses are most attractive and very picturesque.

Having recovered from my earlier faux pas about Peyton Place, Karleen and I became very friendly and she kindly lent me one of her coats for the weekend, she and I being of a similar size. On the following Monday I bought a very nice coat in a shop in Burlington, a fair sized town some thirty miles west of Barre. We stayed several days in Vermont, during which time we were entertained and taken to various places of interest, including the Shelburn Museum with its interesting collection of buildings and artefacts. The museum is in a beautiful area by Lake Champlain, which separates Vermont from New York State. Bud taught me how to shoot with a pistol. It was the first time I'd held a handgun and I nearly shot myself in the foot! It was quite an experience and one I would not care to repeat.

Whilst we were in Vermont Karleen drove us across the border into Canada, where we visited a small town whose name I can't remember. I do remember that we stopped for a meal at a Chinese restaurant and that when we got back that night I did not feel very well and went to bed early. In the morning I found my fellow travellers had also been unwell and we had to conclude that the Chinese meal was the culprit. We were also taken to visit the family's 'camp', a cabin on the shore of a lake not far from Barre. It was a beautiful, peaceful spot and Bill took several colour slides, including some of me playing with the dogs.

At the conclusion of our visit to the Lamsons we were again driven to Burlington past the Trapp Family Lodge. It was here that the family, made famous by *The Sound of Music*, settled after their escape from Austria. It is said that they chose this location because it reminded them of their homeland. In Burlington we picked up a rental car, which we had pre-booked in England. The car was a white Oldsmobile Cutlass with less than one hundred miles on the clock. Although big by present-day standards, it gave a lovely firm ride, unlike the sponginess that had tended to characterise American automobiles that Bill had driven on earlier visits. Thus we started on the journey of over six hundred miles to Cleveland.

We visited Niagara Falls on the way and stayed overnight in a Howard Johnson hotel near Geneva, Ohio, where we decided to break our journey in order to make an early start on the last leg of this part of our tour. Geneva is only about thirty miles from Willoughby, a suburb of Cleveland, which was our objective. The next morning we left Geneva for Willoughby. The journey, though short compared to the distances we had already covered, was rather tedious. Euclid Avenue, a main road into Cleveland which runs through Willoughby, is a very, very long road with many intersections, most of which are controlled by traffic lights suspended above the carriageway. The distinctive appearance of these signals has always stuck in our minds and every time Bill and I see a suspended traffic light, fairly rare in England, we exclaim 'Euclid!' We finally arrived at the Hendersons' apartment and at last Louise and I, who had become so familiar to one another by correspondence, would actually meet face to face!

I suppose it is natural for anyone meeting people for the first time to feel nervous but in this case we certainly had no need. Louise and her husband Henry (usually called Harry) greeted us as though we had known them for years and we soon fell into a close camaraderie. Louise told us that she is usually called 'Honey' and asked us to use that name. I suppose it must have been quite a novelty for them to meet a niece from another country and they asked us many questions about our life in England. They also expressed a lot of interest in the research work I had carried out and which had finally led to this visit.

We were introduced to Louise and Harry's two youngest sons, Steven and John and were told about their daughter Pat, their eldest child, who lived with her husband, another Bill, in Michigan. Between Pat and Steven was another son, Allan. We told them of our own son and daughter, Howard and Mary.

After lots of talking we had a pleasant meal prepared by Honey, who proved to be a keen and gifted cook. After our meal it was suggested that Harry should drive us over to visit Georgia in her apartment on the far side of Cleveland. We agreed and off we set. Georgia was expecting us and we were warmly welcomed with what we had come to recognise as real American hospitality. I was immediately struck by the similarity of Georgia's looks to those of my sisters, particularly the younger one, Pat and, to a somewhat lesser extent, my mother.

Georgia could not have been nicer to us, which I found rather surprising considering the circumstances that had led to our meeting. She told me quite a lot about my father and it was obvious that she had been very fond of him and still was, despite the revelation of his secret. I was relieved that she took everything in such a big-hearted way and seemed to bear no malice toward me. We were taken to visit Georgia's daughter, Dorothy, who lived nearby with her children. I had the feeling that Dorothy, unlike her mother, was slightly hostile to me, but that was quite understandable given the situation. It may be that wives are more broadminded about their husband's transgressions than are daughters about their father's.

Back in the Willoughby home plans were made for the next day. Doris, Louise's eldest sister, and her husband, Harold, would come and visit. I expected that to be very interesting as Doris, being the eldest sister of the family and of a similar age to my mother, could perhaps tell me more about the time of my mother's sojourn in the United States and the deception that followed her departure. In the event one little snippet of information did emerge, which was that my mother assisted Doris in her plan to elope with her boyfriend in order to marry him against the wishes of her parents! Doris and my mother must have had similar temperaments and a great sense of the dramatic.

As well as this, Doris proved to be a mine of general information and told me that the family loved my mother very much. They called her 'The Irish Colleen' on account of her lovely complexion and very blue eyes. The one person my mother did not get on with was her sister-in-law, Helen, Guy's wife. Helen was a redhead and had the fiery temperament that some people associate with it. I don't suppose we shall ever know what really prompted my mother not to return to the United States. I am sure it was not just homesickness.

On the third day of our visit I asked Harry if he would take us to visit the birthplace of my elder sister but he declined. He explained that this would involve driving through a part of Cleveland which had acquired a very bad reputation for crime, and he did not think it would be safe, even in a car. At the close of our visit we were told that we would be welcome to come back to Willoughby any time we were in the United States. Honey mentioned that a family reunion was held from time to time. She promised to let us know when the next one was planned and hoped that we would be able to come. After thanking Honey and Harry for their kindness and hospitality, we invited them to come to England and stay with us.

So the day of our return to Boston dawned and we prepared for a long drive. I was in a relaxed and very relieved frame of mind as I pondered on the success of our visit to Henry and Louise. We were going on to see Terry, my English cousin, who now lives in the United States. It is always a pleasure to see Terry and his wife, Joyce. He was, from the age of eleven, brought up by my grandmother on account of the fact that his parents had separated during the war, So my grandmother took him in as well as me, and I came to regard him as a brother. We both had a happy and contented few years together in a stable family atmosphere. My grandmother must have been an absolute brick and I loved her dearly. She was very strict with us, which, perhaps, was a good thing.

My grandmother gave me a great feeling of security and love and I am sure the same goes for Terry. When he grew up and married he lived in London for a while but, not being very successful there, he decided to seek his fortune overseas. First he went to Canada and then in the United States where the family settled happily in South Weymouth, a small town near Cape Cod in the Commonwealth of Massachusetts.

After leaving Willoughby we travelled for most of the day on the Interstate highway. Although this is a superb road it can become somewhat boring and we decided to divert into the Adirondack Mountain area to the north of the main road. The scenery in the Adirondack National Park is very beautiful and we found a delightful little motel in a place called Indian Lake. We stayed overnight and then returned to the Interstate highway. Our excursion into the byways reminded us of the claim of South Africa to be 'a world in one country'. I think that could also apply to the United States. There's such a variety of scenery, and each state has its individuality – mountains, wide open prairies and lakes – in fact, there's something to suit everybody vacation-wise. There is really no need for our American friends to leave their shores, but I suppose one reason for them to come to Europe is to soak up the history and maybe, like me, to trace their roots!

We finally arrived at Terry's house and were warmly welcomed by both Terry and his wife, Joyce. We settled in for a relaxed few days during which we were taken to various places of interest in and around Boston. These included the Paul Revere Freedom Trail, the State Capitol, the Italian Quarter and Cape Cod. We also visited Plymouth, where the Pilgrim Fathers made their first landing in the *Mayflower*. There is a full-size replica of the *Mayflower* in Plymouth that looks so tiny and frail compared with today's ocean going ships. My mind was much exercised by the thought of the pioneers of that adventure into the unknown. The privations they must have suffered in crossing the Atlantic Ocean in a vessel with few amenities and none of the technological aids to passenger comfort, like stabilisers, which we take for granted these days.

The Atlantic Ocean, with its mountainous seas and other hazards, can be a very cruel environment. I believe that sickness and disease were rife during the long voyage and it was truly a case of the survival of the fittest. I am sure that, having survived that crossing, all other adversities would be tackled and beaten.

Whilst in Plymouth we also visited a reconstruction of a settlement depicting the way of life of the early pilgrims. The guides were dressed in the clothes of the period and gave us an insight into the daily living of those days. Life must have been tough but nothing compared with the sufferings and dangers of the journey out. We saw demonstrations of contemporary methods of preparing food and cookery, and the preparation of medicines including pill rolling. Another exhibit was a working schoolroom with pupils and a teacher dressed in the fashion of the time. I came away with the impression of a united and well-organised community with each individual doing specific jobs which suited his or her particular talents.

At last the day arrived for our return to England after a

very eventful and successful visit. Terry took us to the airport and we were on our way home.

My next visit to my American 'family' was in April 1973 and came about through a number of circumstances. Bill had an invitation to visit business associates in Los Angeles; Mary, our daughter, was nearing the end of a working holiday in Australia and would be returning by the Pacific route via Los Angeles, and Howard, our son, had plans to visit Karl and tour the South-Eastern states with him. We decided to fly to Los Angeles, meet Mary there and then drive across the States to Cleveland, where we would visit Louise and Harry in Willoughby. Howard, in the meantime, would fly to the East Coast and meet up with Karl, who would drive them to Willoughby via the South-Eastern States. This way we would all meet together.

The day arrived and we boarded our flight to Los Angeles via New York. We arrived at about the same time as Mary's flight – from the other side of the world – landed.

We were met by a business associate of Bill's, from one of the Hollywood companies that he would be visiting. As we had to pick up the rental car we had booked at the airport Bill's friend suggested that he should lead us to our hotel, also pre-booked, in the San Fernando Valley region, about half an hour's drive away. We duly collected our car, which was a very recent model and made warning noises until all the seat belts were secured. This was something new to us and rather disconcerting, particularly as we were very tired after our long flights.

Bill's friend led the way out of the airport and we followed. The road we had to take was only a very short distance from the airport exit but on the opposite side of the road, so we had to cross six lanes of traffic in what seemed a few yards. We proceeded at what appeared to us to be enormous speed in the wake of our leader's Thunderbird – a car fully living up to its name! We arrived at our hotel, tired but happy to be together. It was lovely to see Mary again and in such good spirits. She had had a wonderful time in Australia and we were regaled with accounts of her activities and adventures.

The next day, after a good night's sleep, we got down to planning our itinerary for the next few weeks, mapping out routes and places to visit on our journey to Cleveland, where we would meet with Howard and Karl at the Hendersons' apartment in Willoughby. The immediate plan was to spend a few days in Los Angeles. Bill's associates had planned a 'Ladies' Programme' for Mary and me while Bill was discussing business with them. Los Angeles is the host to many international conferences and meetings, and the entertainment of spouses while their partners are busy has become a fine art. Sometimes Bill was free and able to join us as, for example, when we were taken to 'Farmers' Market' where all sorts of exotic produce from all parts of the world is sold. Bill also came with us to the Hollywood Bowl, a huge amphitheatre which is the home of a major symphony orchestra. It is very much associated with the name of the conductor, Leopold Stokowski.

Mary and I were taken to Graumann's Chinese Theatre in Hollywood where the footprints of famous film stars are cast in the concrete sidewalk. One evening we were invited to dinner at the home of the owner of a film company. The house was in Beverly Hills, a very exclusive location, and was quite sumptuous (a most desirable residence). We had a splendid dinner and a most enjoyable time with the family. On another evening we were taken out to dinner at a rather super restaurant by a charming young couple. There was a slight embarrassment because Mary, who had been backpacking in Australia, was rather short of formal clothes; but she did have one particular pair of good trousers. As she got up to leave the restaurant the zip went and she had to be escorted between our hosts and us! They, however, took it in good part, and the evening was great fun and thoroughly enjoyed.

We were given tickets for Universal City where we saw mock cowboy fights, and the techniques for film effects were demonstrated and explained. One could have spent a whole day there and not been bored. We had also been given tickets for Disneyland which included entry to all the rides. We decided to leave our hotel and travel to Santa Ana, the district where Disneyland is located, before starting on our long journey east. And so we left Los Angeles and Hollywood. All in all a most enjoyable few days, thanks to the wonderfully generous hospitality of our hosts.

Arrived in Santa Ana we spent a whole day in the Theme Park and enjoyed it immensely. I was most impressed by the cleanliness and orderliness of everything, despite the hordes of visitors. We left Santa Ana early the following morning and set off across the Nevada Desert for Las Vegas. We had been told that on no account must we miss this 'gambling heaven'. We resisted the temptation to risk our slender resources and instead enjoyed a very good meal and then drove around enjoying the sights of this brilliantly lit oasis in the desert. We booked into a motel and I shall always remember switching on the television and seeing President Richard Nixon reassuring the American people of his integrity. It was at the time of the Watergate scandal and he was impeached shortly afterwards. I later asked some Americans if they were surprised. They replied, 'You don't think he's called "Tricky Dicky" for nothing!'

We must have made an early start from Las Vegas, as I remember stopping at a diner in Boulder City, at the border with Arizona, for breakfast. A little further on is the Hoover Dam, a truly very impressive sight – man-made. An even more impressive sight, and entirely natural, is the Grand Canyon, which we reached later in the morning after taking a diversion from the main Interstate highway. The detour was well worthwhile. The canyon is an enormous gorge over two hundred miles long and, in parts, some six thousand feet deep. It has been cut into the rock over millions of years by the flow of the Colorado River, leaving the rock strata exposed in a fantastic variety of patterns. We stayed overnight in a tourist cabin on the rim of the canyon. Our journey back onto the main highway took us through the Painted Desert, so called because of the coloured sands.

Another canyon, much smaller than its 'Grand' brother, particularly impressed me, a perfect scaled-down version which one could take in at a single glance. Back on the Interstate highway once more we entered the Petrified Forest National Park where timber of great antiquity has absorbed minerals until it has virtually been turned to stone. Alongside the road one sees groups of indigenous 'Indian' traders, mostly from the Navajo and Hopi tribes, which are native to this area. They offer for sale all sorts of hand-crafted items but they specialise in working with silver and turquoise.

Over the State boundary now into New Mexico our next port of call was to be Albuquerque, where Bill had a date to visit Sandia Laboratories, a Government-run research organisation. Bill wanted to get details of a development that he thought might be of use in his own kind of work. Despite this being a high security establishment, we were treated with great courtesy and Bill was given a demonstration of the device he was interested in.

On returning to the main road – Albuquerque lay a few miles to the north – we called at a roadside petrol station. This was one of a chain of filling stations cum coffee shops called 'Stuckie's' that were dotted at intervals along the Interstate highways. Having filled the tank, we found the car would not restart; the battery was obviously quite flat. Some American cars at that time had a meter to indicate whether the battery was charging or discharging. Bill had noticed that the meter did not show a charge, but being unfamiliar with the car had assumed that this was because the battery was fully charged.

In fact the meter was right and Bill was wrong! He telephoned the rental company but was told that there was no agent for this make of vehicle in the neighbourhood. They promised to ring around and try to fix something. They did call back after a few minutes and advised that a breakdown truck, known colloquially there as a 'wrecker', would come out from a nearby town called Santa Rosa to tow us to a garage. Although not an official agent for our make of car, they would diagnose and if possible put right, the fault.

The garage in Santa Rosa soon found that the trouble was due to a faulty alternator, but they did not have a replacement. They agreed to put one on order forthwith but until it arrived – they hoped this would be the next day – we were stuck. We were recommended to a motel where we duly repaired. The hotel management could not have been kinder or more helpful. I suppose we had a certain curiosity value, as Santa Rosa is off the main road and I don't suppose they had many visitors from out of the state, let alone from a foreign country thousands of miles away.

After an excellent Mexican-style meal in a nearby restaurant and a good night's sleep, Bill set off to the garage, which was within easy walking distance of the motel, to see what progress in getting a spare had been made. They had located two sources, one in Albuquerque where we had been the day before, and one in a town with the lovely Indian name of Tucumcari to the east of Santa Rosa. Replacements had been ordered from both sources and would be coming on the next Greyhound bus, which was expected fairly soon. This is where the drama began! The bus duly arrived but it was coming from the wrong direction. We waited for the next. Right direction this time, but still no alternator. This performance was repeated until the last bus had come and gone.

Bud, Karleen and dogs, Chelsea, 1961

With Karl and dog, 1969

At Niagara Falls, 1969

Henry and Louise, 1969

With Bill on Mayflower, Plymouth, Mass. 1969

Mary in the Nevada Desert, 1973

The Grand Canyon, 1973

With Navajo Trader, 1973

With Howard and Phyllis at Phyllis's house in Portsmouth,
New Hampshire, 1973

The Statue of Liberty, 1979

With Madeline and El in Abingdon, Mass. 1976

Bud's sundown
ceremony, 1979

With Bud, Karleen and Bill in Vermont, 1979

A Cleveland river trip with John, Mary Ann and Billy, 1988

The Wirsberg Fire Service parade, 1994

Rothenburg-ob-der-Tauber, 1994

The next day, anticipating a probable repeat of the previous day's delay, Bill talked with the workshop foreman to see if there was anything that could be done to effect a repair without a replacement part. Cars had only recently been fitted with alternators in place of the old dynamos, and not a lot was known about them. Asked if they had had many cases of failure, the foreman replied by opening a cupboard full of 'dead' units. An alternator consists of two parts: one that goes round – appropriately called the 'rotor' – and one that stays still, the 'stator'. It was agreed that if the faulty part on our alternator could be identified and replaced with a good one from the 'graveyard', the resulting complete unit should work. It did work; the unit was replaced under the bonnet – sorry, 'hood' in America – and we went on our way, rejoicing, but not before thanking everyone for their help and kindness.

Good things can come out of adversity, and this was a case in point. If things had gone normally we would never have thought of visiting this tiny out of the way town and we would have missed a really great experience.

Back on the Interstate once again, we crossed into Texas and made an overnight stop at a Howard Johnson Inn near Amarillo. From Texas the Interstate runs through Oklahoma and Arkansas to Tennessee. As we were nearing Memphis, Tennessee Bill noticed that the battery was again not charging. We knew that the car rental company had a depot in Memphis Airport, and we decided to go there and try to get a replacement car. Arriving at the airport, Bill went into the car rental depot to negotiate while I waited outside. The policeman on duty asked me to drive round the airport perimeter road as I was in a restricted parking area. I explained that I was unfamiliar with the airport and he agreed to me staying if I moved the car from time to time. Finally Bill reappeared with the good news that a replacement car, of the same type as the one we had, was

available. We reloaded our luggage into the new car and off
we went.

From Memphis we drove to Nashville and then north
across Kentucky to Ohio, passing by Cincinnati, Columbus
and Akron to Cleveland and finally to our meeting place in
Willoughby, where we were warmly greeted by Louise and
Harry. Although we had enjoyed our travels enormously it
was great to settle down for a few days in a relaxed
atmosphere. Now feeling thoroughly at home, Mary asked
for old newspapers as she wished to dye her scuffed shoes.
Request granted! After six months in Australia she had
absorbed the easygoing informality of the country and very
quickly adapted to the homely atmosphere. Howard and
Margaret, his girlfriend, and Karl arrived the next day. It was
good being together again as a family. They had had quite
an extensive tour on their way to Willoughby.

Starting from Boston, Karl drove them via Philadelphia
to Washington D.C. and then on to Roanoke, where they
called on Karl's uncle, Bill Lamson, and his wife, Luz. From
Roanoke they visited Williamsburg and then entered North
Carolina to visit Jamestown. In the last two towns, named
by early settlers after English kings and steeped in colonial
tradition, they saw re-enactments of scenes from the War of
Independence, the 'soldiers' being dressed in the uniforms
of the period and using authentic replica firearms. Whilst in
North Carolina they went to Kitty Hawk where the Wright
brothers, Orville and Wilbur, made the first powered flight.
They continued on the last leg of their journey to
Willoughby, staying overnight at a Holiday Inn.

The adventures of the three were recounted over a meal
on the evening of their arrival. There was not room in the
Hendersons' apartment to accommodate all of us so
Howard, Karl, Mary and Margaret were 'farmed out' to
Aunts Marjorie and Elizabeth, who had fairly spacious
apartments in a condominium in Cleveland. Bill and I

stayed with Louise and Harry. The next morning we prepared for our departure in our separate cars, having said farewell to our hosts and thanking them for their kindness to us.

We had all decided to visit Niagara Falls as Mary had not been there, and I had visited only the American side. Bill, who had seen both the American and Canadian sides, had been very conscious of the difference. Beautifully laid out parkland and immaculately tended gardens on the Canadian side contrasted with the rather drab appearance of the American town at that time. The falls themselves, seen from either side are, of course, absolutely breathtaking.

Karl had to return directly to Vermont and would take Howard and Margaret with him. Bill, Mary and I on the other hand decided to continue through Canada and to visit Montreal before joining up with the others in Barre, Vermont. Before separating, we all had a meal together in a restaurant on the Canadian side. A very fine highway joins Niagara with Montreal, and it did not take us long to reach the city, where we booked into a Holiday Inn hotel for the night.

Next morning we set off for South Barre to stay with Bud and Karleen before driving to Boston to catch our flight home. Howard, Karl and Margaret had arrived the previous day and were already enjoying the Lamson hospitality. Our meal in the evening is well worth a mention, lobster and strawberry shortcake (not together), which is a traditional American standby for feeding visitors. The lobsters had been carefully selected from the local fish dealer and were alive when brought home. Bud, who was a great practical joker and entertainer, asked me if I knew how to hypnotise a lobster. Knowing him also to be a tease, and suspecting some sort of trick, I answered warily that I did not but was sure he would show me how. He was quite serious, however, and proceeded to demonstrate. He set the lobster on the draining board, being careful to avoid the menacing claws, and began to stroke its back. It really worked and the lobster became absolutely still and calm. I felt a small twinge of conscience feeling we had lulled it into a false sense of security, knowing we planned to eat it that evening…

After an excellent meal, the younger members of the family went off to an open-air cinema nearby. On the way back they had a problem with the car's lights, which delayed their return. Karl was much taken with Mary and annexed her for most of the remaining time, canoeing on their lake and generally entertaining her. It was getting near time for Bill to return to work, but we did have a day to spare before our flight was due to leave Boston for England. We decided, therefore, to make a slight detour and visit Portsmouth, New Hampshire, where Bud's sister, Shirley, and her husband, Dick, lived.

After saying our goodbyes to Bud and Karleen we all set off for Portsmouth. Karl drove Howard, Mary and Margaret, and Bill and I followed in our rented car. In Portsmouth we met not only Shirley and Dick but also Dick's aunt, Phyllis. Bill and I had already met Phyllis when she came to England, some years previously, on her way back from Russia. On that occasion she was accompanied by her niece, Marilyn, who had been visiting a penfriend in England. Marilyn, now grown up, was also in Portsmouth, and we were pleased to renew our acquaintance with her. Phyllis was a very intrepid lady, a retired schoolteacher who spoke fluent Russian and had travelled extensively.

Bill and I stayed overnight with Shirley and Dick but Karl, with Howard, Mary and Margaret, went on to Boston where they intended to do some sightseeing before Mary flew back to England. Howard and Margaret took the train to New York City before flying home. Bill and I now started on the last leg of our long and eventful journey and I had time to reflect on what had been achieved. I had now collected one stepmother, one half-sister, six aunts and numerous cousins and more distant relatives; all for the price of a few postage stamps and a lot of perseverance! I had also travelled some four thousand miles in the United States and Canada, and passed through thirteen states and two Canadian provinces. In Boston, at last, we returned the car and boarded our flight back to England.

In the autumn of 1979, Bill had to attend a conference in Los Angeles and we decided that I would travel with him to New York. We would spend a few days in Manhattan, rent a car and then drive to New Hampshire and Vermont. After that we would travel to Boston where I would visit Terry and Joyce. Bill would put on his 'business hat' and fly on to California.

Carrying out our plan we accordingly arrived at New York's JFK Airport. We took a taxi to the Hilton hotel in downtown Manhattan, where we had a reservation. I remember it rained very heavily on the first day, but despite that we explored the city thoroughly, and largely on foot. A colleague of Bill's had strongly recommended that we visit the Frick Museum. We did so and found it absolutely delightful. A conducted tour, which included Wall Street, the famous financial district, and Chinatown, which I thought was very scruffy, took us to Battery Park at the southernmost tip of Manhattan Island. From Battery Park we travelled by boat to the Statue of Liberty, which stands on an island in the bay which separates New York from New Jersey.

We ate very well in Manhattan, either in the hotel's excellent restaurant, called Hurlingham, or in places with names that appealed to us. In no case were we disappointed with our choice. New York is a very cosmopolitan city and reflects the culture of many nations. I particularly remember a Hungarian restaurant that compared very well with a favourite haunt of ours in London's Soho.

We had already booked a rental car and we collected this before leaving Manhattan. From New York we drove across Connecticut and then through Rhode Island (the smallest State in the US) to Massachusetts. Here we aimed for a town called Abington, about thirty miles south of Boston. I will interrupt the narrative now to explain our reason for visiting Abington.

Some months before our trip I had received, quite out of the blue, a letter from one Madeline Turner, who claimed to be the daughter of my father's brother, Guy, and therefore a first cousin of mine. She had not been mentioned to me before either by Louise or any of the other relatives and even now I don't know how she had found my name and address. Apparently she had heard, presumably on the 'grapevine', that I had been researching the Lamson family and decided to contact me directly.

Madeline, who was a widow, lived in a large, detached house in a pleasant residential area. A self-contained suite in the house was let to a retired architect, a widower named Eldridge, 'El' for short. He and his late wife had been close friends of Madeline and her husband. Madeline told us about her background and varied interests, which included watercolour painting and antique collecting. In fact she still ran a small and exclusive antique business.

El talked about his experiences as an architect in South America, where he had been involved in the design of major hospital schemes. He showed us photographs of some of these projects. While Madeline prepared food for us El acted as barman producing, with great skill and professionalism, magnificent cocktails including my favourite, a daiquiri: quite the best daiquiri I have ever tasted.

Madeline's son and daughter lived not very far away, and during our stay we visited them both. The son, Curtis – 'Curt' for short – and his wife, Dene, lived on a small farm outside the town. The daughter, another Marilyn, and her husband lived in a house not far from Madeline's and in the same general area. Madeline had another son, Ken, whom we did not meet.

We thoroughly enjoyed our stay with Madeline and our visits to her son and daughter. We promised to keep in touch. We told Curtis, who is in banking and makes periodic business trips to Europe, that we would be delighted to entertain him any time he was in England. I am pleased to say that he has taken us up on this offer several times since then. We are always delighted to see him and exchange news about our families.

It was now time to move on, bearing in mind that our stay in New England was limited by Bill's schedule, and we set out for our next port of call, which was to be Bud and Karleen's home in Vermont. It was good to be with Bud and Karleen again and to enjoy their excellent hospitality. Bud was in his usual good form and entertained us with an account of all that had happened since our last meeting. He amused us by performing a typically American 'Sundown Ceremony'. This involved lowering the Stars and Stripes flag, which flew proudly over their land, and firing a small cannon installed specifically for this purpose.

From South Barre we drove to Portsmouth to stay with Shirley and Dick. One evening they took us to a restaurant called the Pilot House in Rye, a coastal town about ten miles south of Portsmouth. The restaurant is set in a vast area of reeds which are illuminated at night. The view from the dining room is one of the most beautiful I think I have ever seen. After our meal Dick and Shirley took us back to their house in Portsmouth where we spent the night before carrying on to Boston.

At Logan Airport, Bill, after some delays, caught a flight to Los Angeles. Terry met me at the airport and drove me to their home in South Weymouth where I spent a few happy days before returning to the airport for my flight back to

England. During the long flight I had time to reflect on the events of the past few weeks and I felt very gratified at having been accepted, with such sincerity, into my father's family.

Arriving back at Heathrow I picked up our car from the long-term car park and proceeded homewards. It was not, as I had hoped, a twenty-minute journey, but a good two hours. There had been an accident on the motorway, which had been closed, and vehicles were diverted onto the ordinary road, which, slow at the best of times, was now brought almost to a standstill by the extra traffic. It was a beautiful Indian summer day, but I was much too hot and tired to appreciate it.

Home at last, I found that life had been going on quite happily and efficiently without me, so I settled down to the daily round, the common task, and looked forward to Bill's return from LA.

★

Nine years were to elapse before my next visit to the United States but that did not mean that contact with my family was lost. The traffic now tended to be in our direction. A letter from Louise informed me that she and Henry planned to visit England and asked if they could stay with us. The trip was planned by their family as a treat to celebrate their parents' fiftieth wedding anniversary. We had now moved from our flat in West London to Taplow, a picturesque village near Maidenhead in Buckinghamshire, which was within easy reach of the airport and London and would make a good centre for touring. I promptly wrote to Louise to say that we would be delighted to put them up as long as they wished. It would be a good opportunity to return some of the wonderful hospitality they had shown us.

The day of Louise and Henry's arrival dawned and we

drove to Heathrow Airport to meet them. On the way Bill and I thought it would be a good idea to suggest to them that we should visit an historic house, Dorney Court, as it lies more or less on the route back from the airport. It seemed to us that this would make an interesting introduction to Buckinghamshire and indeed to the English scene. I think they did enjoy the visit, but looking back with hindsight, maybe it was not such a good idea to take two weary travellers around a place of interest when they must have been very tired and jet-lagged. However, we all arrived home at last. They must have been very relieved but were obviously too polite to say so.

The next day we took our visitors, now thoroughly rested, on a general tour of exploration. I cannot remember now, in detail, the exact route we took, but I do recall visiting Hampton Court and Windsor Castle and taking a sightseeing tour around London. Henry shared Bill's love of walking and they would spend hours strolling in Maidenhead and along the river bank. During their visit with us Louise mentioned that she hoped to organise a family reunion at some time in the future. Bill and I said we would like to participate and Louise promised to advise us of the date and venue.

The next family member to visit us was Bud Lamson's sister Shirley Hodgdon. She had come over with the intention of researching her mother's family. Her mother's maiden name was Halsey. The Halseys originated in Alderney but finally settled in Newent, Gloucestershire. She had planned quite a full itinerary and we did our best to help. First we paid a visit to the village of Ridgewell in Essex, where the three Lamson brothers lived before they sailed for America all those years ago. Shirley hoped that maybe she might find some trace of them, but of course nothing was found, as there were no records before the seventeenth century, the time of the Puritan movement – 1603 to 1649 – which precipitated the exodus of many to 'the New World'.

On our way to Newent we made a detour to the American Museum in Claverton Manor near Bath, which houses many interesting documents and artefacts. We went on to Newent. On another occasion we drove Shirley to Southampton Airport for her flight to Jersey.

I now heard from Louise that a date had been fixed for the proposed reunion party she had mentioned when we last met. She and Harry had moved from Cleveland to Easton, Illinois, where they were living on a farm inherited from Harry's mother. Their son, John and his wife, Mary Ann, were still living in the Cleveland area, although they had moved from Willoughby to Lakewood, a suburb to the west of the city. John would be in charge of the organisation of the reunion, which was to be held in a large public park not far from Lakewood.

Bill had retired, so finding time to go to the States presented no problem. We decided that, having crossed the Atlantic, we might as well enjoy ourselves by making a round trip, visiting various people on the way, including Louise and Harry in their new home, and another cousin I have not yet mentioned, Shirley Nelson, who was the daughter of my father's brother, Guy, and lived in Madison, Wisconsin, some 200 miles north of Easton. We planned to finish up in Lakewood for the reunion party. A lot of driving would be involved, but this did not deter Bill or me as we both enjoy travelling in America. We know how to find good places to stop off for refreshments or, where necessary, for an overnight stay.

Having checked with everyone on our visiting list that they would be available – and that it would be convenient to call – we duly set off on a flight to Boston. On arrival at Logan Airport, one item of our baggage failed to appear on the carousel. We reported this and were told that it would be investigated and if we would leave telephone numbers where we could be contacted, they would advise us when they had located the missing item.

We now proceeded to pick up the hire car, which we had booked in advance, and left the city for the short drive to South Weymouth. Here we intended to spend the first day or two of our tour in the relaxing company of Terry and Joyce. Earlier in this account, you may remember, I introduced Terry as the English cousin with whom I had spent much of my childhood when we were both living with my grandmother.

Thoroughly refreshed, we set off for the drive north across Boston to Portsmouth in New Hampshire, where Shirley and Dick Hodgdon were expecting us. As usual we were made very welcome and royally entertained. During this visit Dick, who is a keen and very skilled woodworker, showed us some of the projects he had completed including a superb roll-top desk. Whilst we were with Shirley and Dick we had a call from British Airways to say that our baggage had been located. It had been to Johannesburg and was now on its way back to Boston, from whence it would be brought to us in Portsmouth! It appears that when our baggage was checked in at Heathrow it was noticed that the handle of Bill's fold-over suit carrier was insecure. They fixed it with sticky tape but, unfortunately, the airline label from a previous trip to Johannesburg, which Bill had not removed (naughty Bill) had been read instead of the Boston one. The next day two very courteous and apologetic British Airways representatives arrived by car and ceremoniously handed over Bill's bag.

From Portsmouth we drove to the border with Vermont and then continued westwards to Burlington in the extreme west of the state. Here we paid a visit to one of our earliest American 'finds', Karl Lamson. Karl was now married and we met his wife, Shelley, and his two stepchildren. We were shown over the house and were interested to see that Karl still pursued his hobby of collecting geological samples. He showed us the phial of the famous Alum Bay coloured sands, from the Isle of Wight, that we had sent him years ago.

From Burlington we crossed Lake Champlain, which forms the border with New York State, and drove to Lake Placid where we had a hotel room booked for the night. The next morning we set off on the long trip to Easton, Illinois. The first part of our journey took us south through the beautiful Adirondack National Park. From there we continued south, and then bearing south-west, but still in New York State, we crossed the border into Pennsylvania. Driving all the way across Pennsylvania we entered Ohio, where we stayed the night in the industrial city of Columbus. Our journey next day took us out of Ohio, right across Indiana and finally into Illinois. We could probably have made it to Easton by nightfall but we were becoming distinctly travel weary and would not be the best company for our hosts. The town of Champaign, not far from the Indiana / Illinois border, looked attractive, and we decided to spend the night there.

We were right about Champaign. The town itself was very pleasant and the hotel we chose proved to be extremely comfortable. Now thoroughly fortified and feeling a lot more sociable, we set off on the last stage of this leg of our journey. It was a good thing that we had not tried to reach Easton the night before. Because, once off the Interstate roads, travelling became much slower and I shudder to think how late we would have been. We had thought that, on our previous travels, particularly the trip from Los Angeles to Boston, we had seen just about all the different types of scenery that the USA had to offer but we were wrong. In the central region of Illinois one drives through vast areas of pastureland that seem to have no boundaries. Anyone who has seen the Hitchcock film *North by Northwest* will know what I mean.

We received a great welcome from Louise and Harry who proudly showed us around their new property. You may wonder why we drove all that way when we were scheduled to meet them soon at the reunion. The reason was that they very much wanted us to see their new home and for us to meet Harry's brother and his wife who lived nearby and would not be coming to Cleveland.

Harry and Louise took us to the town of Lincoln, named after Abraham Lincoln before he became president. There is a village here which depicts life as it would have been in Lincoln's day. It made me think of the settlement we had visited near Plymouth, Mass., which showed how the first settlers had lived some two centuries earlier. We were also taken to the Illinois State Museum in Springfield, the state capital, and also to a branch of the museum at Dickson Mounds. This huge burial ground site was excavated by an Archaeologist Dr Don F Dickson, whose name it bears, about fifty years before the time of our visit and shows the remains of some two hundred prehistoric people with their possessions. The site was opened to the public in 1927. In between these visits we called at a large ranch where I was rather upset to see the cattle standing in the blazing mid-June sun light with absolutely no cover. I wondered how the RSPCA would have reacted…

When our few days in Easton came to an end, and after thanking Harry and Louise for their great hospitality, we climbed back into our car and set off north for Wisconsin. Arriving at Janesville we had no difficulty in finding Shirley's house. Here we had another warm reception by Shirley together with her daughter, Carolyn and Carolyn's husband, Denny, whom we had already met when they visited us in England.

From Wisconsin we set off on the final lap for Cleveland. Fortunately our rental car had very effective air-conditioning, in common with most American cars by then, and you did not notice the intense heat until you got out. I remember stopping at a filling station for fuel, and opening the car door was like opening the door to a furnace. We also stopped off at an enormous roadside shopping mall, at the back of nowhere. We had refreshments and I explored the huge shopping areas. I bought a pair of trousers, which turned out to be amongst the nicest I have ever owned. I wish I could go back and get some more but even if we were in those parts again I doubt if I could remember the name of the mall or its exact location.

Arrived at last in Lakewood we were greeted by John, Mary Ann, their children Jim and Annie and their dog, Fred. Harry and Louise arrived shortly after us. Joining us for supper that evening were Mary Ann's father and mother, Bill and Ann Back. It was still very hot and coming from an air-conditioned car to a house without air conditioning made it all the more noticeable. Our meal consisted of lasagne, a very popular dish in America. It looked and smelled most appetising but the heat had taken away my appetite. Bill Back, sitting next to me at the table, kept coaxing me to eat – but with little success. Towards the end of a lively discussion on all sorts of topics the talk turned to the subject of researches into family backgrounds. Although Bill Back was born in America, his family came originally from a village in north West Germany called Damme; he had never been to Germany and would love to go there and visit Damme. Bill and I said that we would like to come too, and so did John and Mary Ann. So it was agreed that we should plan a trip in the not too distant future.

Next day was the great day for the reunion party and we all repaired to the park where it was to be held. We had a little difficulty in finding the site but we met Louise's daughter, Pat, and her husband, another Bill, who knew the way and we followed them. Louise's three sisters, Doris, Elisabeth and Marjorie were there, and as it was Doris's ninetieth birthday a huge cake had been made in her honour. No alcohol was allowed in the public park so the toast had to be drunk in soft drink. I have an idea that some of the men found a way around this restriction but, as Bill was driving, it did not worry us.

Most of the people at the party we had already met at some time or other but there were exceptions: Betty Perryman, the daughter of my father's sister, Mildred, and therefore a first cousin to me; Raymond, the son of my father's brother, Guy, was totally blind and he and Bill, who works as a volunteer with our local society for blind and partially sighted people, had a lively chat about the difference in facilities between our two countries. Raymond has learned to live with his sight problem and is very independent, but he acknowledges the support he receives from his wife, Joan, whom we also met at the party. After all these years I cannot be sure that I have not missed anybody out. If I have and they happen to read this account I do apologise.

Whilst in the Cleveland area we were taken to the Blossom Music Centre, an open-air concert venue in Cuyahoga Falls south of the city. We heard a programme of classical music played by the legendary Cleveland Orchestra. The atmosphere was terrific and the playing superb. After the concert we went to a vineyard named 'Chalet Debonne' where we sampled wines made from locally grown grapes.

After leaving Cleveland we drove across Pennsylvania and New York State to Massachusetts to visit my cousin Madeline at her house in Abington, to the south of Boston. Madeline, who had not been at the reunion party, made us very welcome as before, and we also met her friend El, the retired architect, again. After drinks, poured by El in very generous measures, we went out to dine at a nearby restaurant serving the most superb steaks. We stayed overnight at Madeline's and the next morning went for a long walk around Abington with her and El before driving to the airport to catch our flight home.

★

Our next trip to the United States was tentatively planned for 1992, when Harry would be celebrating his eightieth birthday. In the meantime however, we received two pieces of news, one sad and the other a matter of joy. The sad news was that Mary Ann's father, Bill, had died; the good news was that Mary Ann was to have another baby. Clearly Mary Ann's father's death had reduced the incentive for our proposed trip to Germany, but Mary Ann did not think we should abandon the idea entirely. Obviously we would have to wait until the new arrival was old enough to travel.

We did travel to Cleveland in 1992. Delta Airlines now flew from Gatwick to Cleveland with just a short stop at Detroit on the way. We picked up a rental car at Cleveland Airport and set out in torrential rain for John and Mary Ann's new house in Lakewood. We had not been there before and had to stop off at a shop to ask the way. We eventually found the address and were welcomed by the whole family, including the dog, Fred, who recognised us and greeted us with much tail-wagging. The detached house stood on a tree-lined avenue not far from the lake shore. Henry and Louise were staying as well as Bill and I, but there was plenty of room for us all. After a pleasant evening meal and a good night's sleep we awoke to brilliant sunshine, which augured well for the days celebrations. The party was held in the local yacht club where we had been before with Mary Ann's mother and father.

An excellent repast was provided followed by the usual speeches and toasts. A goodly representation of the Lamson and Henderson families was present and we were able to renew many acquaintances. The day after the party John drove us along the lake shore to the ferry terminal from which boats left for an island called Putin Bay. After a short boat trip we arrived on the island, rented a golf buggy and set off to investigate. Apparently the island had been the scene of fierce fighting in the War of Independence and we saw a re-enactment of a battle scene with actors dressed in the uniforms of the period and actually firing ancient weapons. Annie had come with us and we all voted it a very good day out.

The following day we drove to the other side of Cleveland to visit Steven and Hazel at their home near Willoughby. They lived, together with their son, Brian, and daughter, Stephanie, in a big house in extensive grounds planted with Christmas trees, which they cultivated for sale. We also visited Wally and Betty Perryman, whose daughter, Linda, had visited us, together with two friends, when they were touring in the United Kingdom.

Whilst we were in Cleveland John and Mary Ann took us on a boat trip under the numerous bridges in the harbour area. John and Mary Ann's latest addition to the family, Billy, came with us. He was about two years old then and behaved beautifully. The topic of our proposed visit to Germany came up again and it was decided to organise the trip for the summer of 1994. An itinerary was discussed and we agreed to make the travel arrangements for Europe nearer the date. John and Mary Ann would arrange their flight to Germany through Hazel, John's sister-in-law, at her travel agency.

We returned by Delta from Cleveland but our flight was not as pleasant as our outward journey. Instead of just setting down in Detroit and taking off again without disembarking, as we had on our flight out, we now had to get off the plane and stay in the airport lounge for about an hour. On continuing our flight we found that the seating was very cramped and we were hardly able to sleep at all.

★

As the summer of 1994 approached we began to make detailed plans for our trip. We invited my sister, Pat, who had accompanied us on several foreign trips and particularly liked Germany, to join us in this adventure and she readily agreed. At that time we had a very efficient travel agent in our local village and we asked him to make all our travel arrangements except for the Hendersons' flight and car booking, which they would arrange themselves through Hazel's travel agency. In consultation with John and Mary Ann over the telephone we agreed a route starting in the vicinity of Damme and ending somewhere in easy reach of Frankfurt Airport from which they would fly home.

We decided that we would start our German journey on the fourth of June, and having decided on the towns and cities we wished to visit we asked our travel agent to find and, if we agreed with his choice, to book hotel accommodation. John, Mary Ann and their three children would fly to Frankfurt, pick up their rental car and drive on the autobahn to our chosen hotel in the Damme area. Having regard to the estimated time of their arrival, we reckoned that if we crossed on an early ferry, we should all arrive at about the same time.

We approved a draft itinerary which our travel agent submitted, and asked him to confirm the hotel bookings. It was now 'all systems go', and all we had to do was to advise John and Mary Ann and wait for the fourth of June.

We picked up my sister and made for the ferry port at Dover. Once over the Channel we started on the long trek across France, Belgium and Holland to Germany. On the advice of our travel agent we had decided not to go directly to Damme but to stop off at a hotel a short drive away, which had easy access from the motorway. We arrived late afternoon or early evening and I think John and Mary Ann were already there or arrived very soon after we did. John was very bucked to have been upgraded from the Volkswagen Passat, which he had ordered, to a beautiful black Mercedes. We rather thought that his sister-in-law had something to do with this!

The hotel we stayed in that first night was the Hotel Bitter at a place called Wallenhorst. The next morning we set off, fully refreshed, to explore Damme and to find our next hotel, which proved to be a little way out of the actual village at a tiny place called Dümmerlohausen. The name of the family-run hotel was Hotel Schomacher. It was very comfortable and pleasant and the proprietress was most helpful. In the evening, after we had eaten, Mary Ann commandeered the payphone to follow up various leads she had with regard to her father's family.

The next day Mary Ann, John and the children went off to explore the surrounding countryside and to follow up certain leads yielded by Mary Ann's telephone calls the previous evening. Bill, Pat and I also looked around the area and ended up at the side of a local lake. There was a very attractive cafe where we sat at an outside table in glorious sunshine and had lunch. That evening the restaurant in our hotel was closed. It is common practice in Germany for smaller hotels to have one 'rest day' per week when no food is served after breakfast, and this happened to be the day. We were not downhearted, however, as we had noticed a very nice-looking restaurant along the road, so we went there and were not disappointed.

The following day we were back on the autobahn again, this time heading east towards the Hartz Mountains. We had arranged to stay in a town called Braunlage, which is a ski resort in winter and a walking and sporting paradise in summer. We had booked to stay in a hotel where Bill and I had stayed on several previous occasions named 'zur Tanne' (the Fir Tree Inn). Zur Tanne was up to its usual excellent standard, and after freshening up after a fairly long journey we repaired to the restaurant. Mountain air certainly sharpens the appetite and we were able to do justice to the wide range of dishes, including regional specialities, which the menu had to offer.

The following day we explored the town before setting off for our next port of call – which was to be Berlin. Braunlage lies to the south of the main Hannover-Berlin autobahn and we decided to take a cross-country route which would bring us back onto the autobahn near Magdeburg, thereby 'cutting off the corner' and saving us quite a lot of mileage. It also had the attraction to Bill and me of taking us into an area that had been in the East Zone and which, on previous visits we had seen only through binoculars across the border fortifications.

Arriving in Berlin we drove straight to our hotel, the Alsterhof in Augsburger Strasse just off the principal shopping street in the western part of the city, the famous Kurfürstendamm. We had no difficulty finding our objective. We had good maps and the street names are clearly marked. We had been allocated rooms quite near to each other on an upper floor. In previous visits to Berlin, Bill and I had been surprised at the size of rooms in hotels near the city centre, and this was no exception. Actually the room occupied by Bill and me was larger than the one shared by John and Mary Ann and their children, but the latter had better facilities for a family. We all ate that night in the hotel restaurant and retired early in preparation for the following day's sightseeing.

Berlin is a big city with an excellent underground railway system, but a lot of the central part can be covered on foot. There are also tour buses that depart frequently from the Kurfürstendamm and take in what used to be the Eastern

Sector. I was rather tired after all our travelling and did not feel up to an extensive tour of the city, particularly remembering Bill's tendency to embark on marathon walks. It was therefore agreed that on the first day of our visit Bill, John, Mary Ann and the three children should go without me.

Mary Ann loves museums and they decided to visit Museum Island, which is located on the north side of Unter den Linden, where the river splits in two. One of the museums on the island houses the Pergamon Altar, which was brought to Berlin in the nineteenth century and reassembled in a specially constructed building. It's a thrilling sight, and Bill says even the children were enthralled. Bill now went into marathon mode and persuaded the party to walk all the way to the Brandenburg Gate at the end of Unter den Linden and then, across a vast sea of bomb damage rubble, to Potsdamer Platz where there is an underground station. Even Bill admits that he almost began to regret his decision as Potsdamer Platz seemed to recede more and more into the distance. Finally, back at the hotel, tired and a little footsore, they were eager to regale me with an account of their day.

The following day we all went out to explore the city further including visits to major department stores, the Ka-De-We (pronounced 'kar-de-vay'), and Wertheim, where John and Mary Ann were able to buy presents to take home to the States. We finally ended up at the Europa Centre, a huge post-war development within easy walking distance of our hotel that houses many shops and restaurants. Having walked around for a while and looked at a number of restaurants we finally found one that appealed to us and which had a free table large enough to accommodate, in comfort, the six of us. Despite the rather unfamiliar menu the children seemed happy with their choices and did full justice to them.

After Berlin we had planned, in our itinerary, to go south to the old walled town of Rothenburg ob der Tauber in Bavaria, which is of particular interest to Americans, for reasons that I will explain later. On looking at the map, however, we decided that the distance was too great to cover in one bite, and we decided to look for somewhere to stay overnight about halfway. Bill and I had often used hotels belonging to a chain known as Romantik Hotels and had always found them excellent. There was a Romantik Hotel listed in a village called Wirsberg in the very beautiful scenic area of Franconian Switzerland. This was at just about the right distance, and we asked our travel agent to book rooms.

It was interesting to drive south along the autobahn in what had been East Germany and to observe the enormous variations in the condition of the carriageway between the sections that had been refurbished and those still in the state they had been in before re-unification. Off the autobahn and now on winding lanes we had no difficulty finding Wirsberg and the Romantik Hotel Post, which was more or less in the centre of the village. It was one of the most delightful family-run country hotels that we have visited in Germany or, for that matter, anywhere else, and John and Mary Ann were entranced.

It so happened that at the time of our visit to Wirsberg the village was hosting a rally by all the fire brigades of the area and we were able to witness a parade of firemen through the village streets with bands and dancing children. It was a wonderful sight and one we would not have missed for worlds. I must say that we left Wirsberg with reluctance and all of us hope to have the opportunity to go back some day. It really is a little jewel.

Our onward journey took us to Würzburg where we stopped briefly to see the bridge over the River Main with its statues, and the great Marienberg Castle on the hills above. On arrival at Rothenburg ob der Tauber, we found that there was no access for vehicles into the city during the day. We found a car park and Bill walked to the hotel where we were booked to seek advice. He returned and led us through a special route to the hotel car park. In the hotel 'zur Glocke' (the Bell Inn) we were warmly greeted by the friendly receptionist who showed us to our rooms in the lovely old building. Right opposite was a house, 'am Plönlein' (untranslatable) which has been the subject of many paintings and posters and once featured in a TV advertisement in England. I remember there was a cat sleeping on a window sill, giving a homely touch.

The hotel included a wine shop, and at dinner that night we had a little wine tasting, sampling five or six different wines. We voted unanimously for a wine from Franconia and when we left Bill and I bought six litre bottles to take home with us in the car. I mentioned earlier that Rothenburg is of special interest to Americans. The top of the wall, which almost completely surrounds the city forming a walkway, suffered damage in the Second World War, and repairs were paid for by members of the American Forces whose names, together with the length of the repaired area (in metres), are inscribed beside the areas they adopted, thus, every so often one sees 'Private Jones, 1 m', 'Sergeant Smith, 2 m', and so on.

Rothenburg has an interesting legend dating from the days of the Thirty Years' War. In 1631 the besieging Swedish army, under the command of General Tilly, prepared to take the town, but Mayor Nusch saved the situation by making, and winning, a wager with Tilly that he could drink almost three-quarters of a gallon of wine at a single draught. How much truth there is in this no one knows, but it's a good story and is commemorated by a clock with windows which open every hour, on the hours between 11 a.m. and 10 p.m., to reveal Nusch and Tilly knocking back their steins. The children loved it.

We thoroughly explored the town and its numerous attractions, including a doll and toy museum containing puppet theatres and model rooms dating from 1780 to 1940, and at Christmas time a nativity display. There is also a museum showing medieval torture instruments and their methods of use in olden times. For anyone thinking of visiting this delightful town at Christmas time an added attraction is the Christmas market, held on an open space behind the town hall.

We also drove out into the surrounding countryside to visit, briefly some of the other ancient towns along the 'Romantic Road' (*Romantische Strasse*). One of these, Dinkelsbuhl, is particularly lovely. Although having a similar atmosphere to Rothenburg, it is quite different in a subtle way. It is a town where a photographer could place his or her camera almost anywhere and still get an attractive picture.

Our next, and last, stop was to be in Aschaffenburg, a town within easy reach of Frankfurt Airport and which we had chosen because we believed it typified an ordinary German town, prosperous but virtually without tourists. On the way to Aschaffenburg we deviated from the direct route on the autobahn to visit Mespelbrunn Castle, a little hunting lodge, built on the banks of a small lake in beautiful parkland. We took a conducted tour of the house. This is the sort of place that is pretty well unique to Germany and that is why we included it in our tour.

Arriving in Aschaffenburg we had to find our hotel, which proved none too easy. Bill and I had visited the town before but had always stayed in a different hotel from the one we had booked this time. We were, of course, in two cars, so stopping to ask the way was awkward. However we finally arrived at our target, the Hotel *Wilder Mann* (Wild Man). We realised that we must have passed it at least once on our 'tour' of the town. It was only then that we noticed a big sculpture on the side of the hotel, looking rather like the Tin Man in *The Wizard of Oz*, which, presumably was supposed to represent a wild man. The hotel was very pleasant and comfortable and I would not hesitate to recommend it to anyone coming to Aschaffenburg.

The day of our parting now arrived and we sadly took our farewell of John, Mary Ann, Jimmy, Annie and little Billy. Their company had heightened our enjoyment of the trip and had made us appreciate things that we might not have noticed before. We did not go to the airport with them as we needed get on our way in good time for the long journey ahead of us.

That is a convenient point to close the story I promised to tell. Since our German trip we have kept in touch with John and Mary Ann and the rest of my family. Bill and I have made several trips to the United States for family reunions and birthday celebrations. John and Mary Ann now live in London, where she represents her company. We visit them from time to time. Sometimes John's mother, my aunt Louise, who is now widowed, flies over here to see them, and we all get together.

FIN